Pra

"Adam Miller's *l*
that I didn't like ᵢ
frustrated me because I only wish I had had such a book to
read when I was a 1960s teenager with racing mind and
hormones. And perhaps more poignantly, I wish it had been
available when my children were passing through those difficult and impressionable years. *Letters to a Young Mormon* is
both tender and gentle, and at the same time provocative and
intellectually stimulating. Its disarming honesty is only sur-
passed by the significance of its messages. I recommend it
wholeheartedly, for young and old."

> —ROBERT L. MILLET
> Professor of Religious Education
> Brigham Young University

"These letters read not like missives from a great distance or
from lofty heights, but like the words of a friend who is just
a little further along the road, sending back words of warning, encouragement, and the happy reminder to look at all
the wonders along the path. No trail of breadcrumbs—these
are small bright jewels to mark the way home."

> —KRISTINE HAGLUND
> Editor, *Dialogue: A Journal of Mormon Thought*

"Adam Miller's *Letters to a Young Mormon* is faithful, smart,
witty, well-written, and accessible—the perfect book for any
thoughtful LDS young person."

> —JAMES E. FAULCONER
> Richard L. Evans Professor of Religious
> Understanding
> Brigham Young University

For S.

Letters to a Young Mormon

Adam S. Miller

NEAL A. MAXWELL
INSTITUTE *for*
RELIGIOUS SCHOLARSHIP

Brigham Young University
Provo, Utah

LETTERS TO A YOUNG MORMON
Adam S. Miller

A Living Faith Book

Cover design: Brad Norr
Book design: Joe Bonyata

The paper used in this publication meets the minimum requirements of the American National Standard for Information Sciences—Permanence of Paper for Printed Library Materials. ANSI Z39.48-1984.

ISBN 978-0-8425-2856-6

Printed in the United States of America

maxwellinstitute.byu.edu

Contents

This book is composed as a series of letters. The letters are meant for a young Mormon who is familiar with Mormon life but green in their faith. I imagined myself writing these letters to my own children and struggled, in relation to how we talk about things at church, to say my own piece about what it means to be—as a Mormon—free, ambitious, repentant, faithful, informed, prayerful, selfless, hungry, chaste, and sealed.

The letters do little to benchmark a Mormon orthodoxy. That work belongs to those called to it. Here, my work is personal. I mean only to address the real beauty and real costs of trying to live a Mormon life. And I hope only to show something of what it means to live in a way that refuses to abandon either life or Mormonism.

Agency

DEAR S.,

I don't know. And what I do know is mostly local, half-framed, and hard to say. You ask some tough questions that lack easy answers. But I don't think that this kind of not-knowing is, in itself, a failure. I think it's just life. And, as Mormons, we can't hide from this not-knowing, because, more than anything else, Mormonism is a way of living rather than dodging life. Part of not dodging life is owning this ignorance.

But it's also true that even if I knew what to say and how to say it, you'd still have to work out the answers for yourself. You must bear wholeheartedly the fact that the work of living your life can't be done by anyone else. This is basic Mormonism. You are an agent loose in the world and, as Paul puts it, you must "work out your own salvation with fear and trembling" (Philippians 2:12 NRSV).

You'll be surprised at how true this is. From the near side of trying, it may look like things have been pretty well mapped out for you. Just stick to the plan.

Memorize your Articles of Faith, get your merit badges signed off, complete your Personal Progress, get good grades, go on a mission, go to the temple, have a family, etc. There may be a few details here and there to handle, but nothing major. You've got a map, you just have to follow it.

But once you get to work, you'll be unnerved by the distance between the neat map in your hand and the rough terrain at your feet. Fighting to coordinate the two, you'll be tempted to throw the whole thing over or, by way of compromise, to sit down and gossip about how great the map is. This latter kind of admiration is often mistaken for a religious life. Perhaps it is religious, but it is no life. Even sound maps are just maps. They are no substitute for real roads.

The gap between theory and practice is often biggest with the simplest things. You've promised to pray, but you'll spend a lifetime learning how to pray. You've promised to study the scriptures, but you'll spend a lifetime learning how to read them. And you've promised to give God everything—your time, your talents, your money—but you'll spend a lifetime learning how to consecrate even a part. You cannot forfeit responsibility for this *how*. You cannot wait for someone else to do them for you. If you do not work things out for yourself, they will never be done. You must learn how to body your religion out into the world with your own fingers and toes, eyes and ears, flesh and bones. This can only be done from the inside out.

You are a pioneer. Life has never before been lived in your body. Everything must be done again, as if for the first time. You are an aboriginal Adam, a primal Eve. You are a Mormon.

My dad is a Mormon. He has always been willing to start from scratch. He was raised in a tiny branch of the church in central Pennsylvania. His mother was a member, his father was not. Though he had reasons enough to go his own way, my father gave himself to the work. He married, he worked three jobs, and he came back to church. He was the first and only member of his family to go to college. He earned a PhD.

When I was four, spurred by a kind of prophetic impulse, he tried his hand at Zion. He left the city and bought a hundred-year-old farmhouse with five acres of field and a broken silo. There was no yard, just grass up to my mother's waist. The roof was tin, the walls were horsehair plaster. No one had used the second story for years. My father embraced it and did things he didn't know how to do. He cleared the ground, he posted barbwire fences, he painted and plumbed and poured concrete. He built a barn and bought dogs and cats and horses and cows. He seeded a garden shaped like a wagon wheel and planted an orchard with fruit trees and grapevines. He paneled a bedroom for me, tucked away at the foot of the attic, and laid a tight brown carpet perfect for Matchbox cars. He made me a bookcase and toy chest out of two-by-fours. He could have settled in and watched TV. He didn't need the grief of shoveling manure. Instead, he and my mother acted in good faith to build with their own hands what we only read about at church.

My life has been shaped by my father's outsized ambition, an ambition made real in both the nails he hammered true and those that bent and were hammered home anyway.

If you give yourself to this work, if you do more than is asked of you, if you get up before your alarm sounds and work out your own salvation, then you will find what Paul found, what my father found, and what I have found. You will find as you "work out your own salvation" that "*it is God* who is at work in you, enabling you both to will and work for his good pleasure" (Philippians 2:12–13 NRSV, emphasis mine). But this discovery, this heart-starting revelation that you are not alone, comes only in doing the work itself. Working, you will find that you are not your own and that God is at work in you. You will find that God, in both rough and subtle ways, is working in and through you to do things you can't do and create things you don't entirely understand.

Working, you'll find grace.

Love,
A.

Work

Dear S.,

I can see myself in you. It is both flattering and scary. I see how much you want to be loved, how hungry you are for acknowledgment and approval. I see how much you want to be great. Wanting love is good and wanting to excel is good. The trouble comes from trying to tie them together. Pursue love and pursue excellence—pursue them with abandon. But you will spoil the joy native to each if you spend your life wanting to be loved *because* you are great.

Love is for its own sake. It works only as a gift, never as a reward. It can't be earned or bartered or insured. It is a grace and it is freely given or not given at all. Uncouple your desire to be loved from your desire to be great. Pursue love by striving to give it rather than possess it. Coupling love and ambition fools us into approaching the whole business backwards. Rather than pursuing love by giving ourselves away, we end up trying to capture love with a new and improved version of ourselves. This sucks the freedom out of love and it sucks the joy out of excellence.

As Mormons, we're often unclear about this. We emphasize the necessity of having faith in God's perfect love, and we hammer home the necessity of getting to work and pursuing excellence. We criticize others for neglecting either the need for faith or the need for work. All the while, laboring zealously in defense of these virtues, we tend to yoke them together in a way that hobbles them both.

You must trust in God's perfect love and you must wear out your life in the pursuit of what is excellent, but if you try to secure God's love through your excellence then, no matter how excellent your work, you will fail. Your work will only become an expression of your failure to trust that God's love for you is already palpable and perfect. Your pursuit of excellence will, ironically, hollow out your faith and, absent this trust, you will become more and more doubtful and afraid. The more desperately "worthy" of love you style yourself, the deader your faith in its graciousness will become. You cannot treat God's love as something to be earned while also trusting that God already loves you perfectly. This strategy belies your faith.

Similarly, no longer shackled by uncertainty and anxiety to your doomed project of capturing love, the joy of ambition, of excellence pursued for its own sake, begins to shine. Work that was only a grinding means to an end gets lit with meaning as an end in itself. Unencumbered by a fear of failing, secure in the perfect love passing through you, you put your shoulder to the wheel, you whistle while you work, and the work itself becomes a more perfect expression of an already perfect love.

This is a lesson I'm still learning. At your age, I was painfully competitive. I was determined to prove—at school, on the court, at church, with girls—that I was better than other people, that I was more worthy of love and admiration. This ambition to prove my worth was a fountain of misery. If I excelled at something, it was never enough. If I failed, I shed fearful tears.

I played basketball. Here, I thought, I'll gather a crowd and prove myself. I worked hard. I drilled. I shot endless free throws. I ran miles. I hit the weights. I started earlier and stayed longer. My sophomore year in high school, we won two of some twenty games. My junior year, we won four. Basketball season was an exercise in public humiliation. I cried. I got frustrated. I got angry. I worked harder. I started even earlier, I stayed even longer. My senior year we won eight games. While our girls team went to the state finals, I never managed a winning record.

But I loved basketball. On the playground on a hot summer afternoon, I was loose and fearless. I would whoop and run and smile. The chain nets sang when I sank a baseline jumper. The joy of pinning a shot to the backboard was ecstatic. On the playground, no one was watching. There was nothing to lose. But with my parents in the stands, with the school gathered on a winter night, I was a knot of inhibitions and short-armed free throws. The scoreboard would tip in the visitor's favor and my face would burn. On midwinter nights in that high school gym, my ambition was not to play basketball.

My ambition was to use basketball as a crowbar for leveraging love. And this, win or lose, is no way to play basketball. In fact, it is no way to do anything.

Work, chained to its outcome, is misery. Do what you can, do it better than you're able, and let things happen as they may. The action, not its fruit, is your business. The outcome is not your concern. If God is going to show himself to you in the work that you shoulder, he will only do so if you've stopped craving an approving audience and, instead, work out your own salvation.

Your life is not a movie. It has no audience and it reaches no climax. There is no soundtrack. There is just you and the work and the people who share the work with you. Love the work for its own sake. "Perfect love casts out fear" (1 John 4:18 NRSV). Fearless in love, set ambition free.

Love,
A.

Sin

DEAR S.,

Being a good person doesn't mean you're not a sinner. Sin goes deeper. Being good will save you a lot
of trouble, but it won't solve the problem of sin.
Only God can do this. Fill your basket with good apples rather than bad ones, but, in the end, sin has as
much to do with the basket as with the apples. Sin
depends not just on your actions but on the story
you use those actions to tell.

Like everyone, you have a story you want your life
to tell. You have your own way of doing things and
your own way of thinking about things. But "my
thoughts are not your thoughts, neither are your
ways my ways, saith the Lord. For as the heavens are
higher than the earth, so are my ways higher than
your ways and my thoughts than your thoughts"
(Isaiah 55:8–9). As the heavens are higher than the
earth, God's work in your life is bigger than the story
you'd like that life to tell. His life is bigger than your
plans, goals, or fears. To save your life, you'll have to
lay down your stories and, minute by minute, day by

day, give your life back to him. Preferring your stories to his life is sin.

Sin is endemic to the story you're always telling yourself about yourself. This story shows up in that spool of judgmental chitchat—sometimes fair, sometimes foul—that, like an off-stage voice-over, endlessly loops in your head. This narration follows you around like a shadow. It mimes you, measures you, sometimes mocks you, and pretends, in its flat, black simplicity, to be the truth about you. This story is seductive. It seems so weightless and bulletproof and ideal. But as a shadow it hides as much as it reveals. You are not your shadow. No matter how carefully you line up the light, your body will never fit that profile. Sin is what happens when we choose our shadows over the lives that cast them. Life is full of stories, but life is not a story. God doesn't love your story, he loves you.

Your story, like everyone's, is a bit of a Frankenstein. Without your hardly noticing or choosing, it gets sewn together, on the fly, out of whatever borrowed scraps are at hand. You may have borrowed a bit from your mother, a bit from a movie you liked, and a bit from a lesson at church. You may have stitched these pieces together with a comment overheard at lunch, a glossy image from a magazine, and a second-grade test score. Whatever sticks. More stuff is always getting added as other stuff is discarded. Your story's projection of what you should be is always getting adjusted. Your idea of your shadow's optimal shape gets tailored and tailored again.

Like most people, you'll lavish attention on this story until, almost unwittingly, it becomes your blueprint for how things ought to be. As you persist in measuring life against it, this Franken-bible of the self will become a substitute for God, an idol. This is sin. And this idolatrous story is all the more ironic when, as a true believer, you religiously assign God a starring role in your story as the one who, with some cajoling and obedience, can make things go the way you've plotted. But faith isn't about getting God to play a more and more central part in your story. Faith is about sacrificing your story on his altar.

Everyone knows that little blush of pleasure that comes when you feel like your life and your story match. And I'm sure you know the pinch of disappointment that follows when you feel like your life hasn't measured up. These blushes and pinches tend to rule our daily lives. They push and pull and bully us from one plot point to the next. "Now I should be this," we say, "now I should have this, now I should do this. . . ." Meanwhile, the pedestrian substance of life gets shuffled offstage in favor of epic shadows.

Think about what it's like when you buy a new shirt. You slip, hopeful, into the dressing room. Backed by doubled mirrors, you model it and ask, "Does this fit my story, does this match my shadow?" As a teenager, I never had much luck with this. In junior high, I grew fast, we didn't have much money, and my clothes never seemed to fit. My sleeves were short and my pants were flooded. I was always yanking at my cuffs, trying to make them longer. Late one fall, my mother took me to buy a new coat. I picked a kind of knockoff ski jacket, bright blue and trimmed with red and green. We even bought it a size too big. When we got home, I put it on and went out for a long, cold walk along our empty country road. For a long time I walked back and forth, back and forth, on a half-mile stretch, imagining with great pleasure what a stranger might say if they saw me, what they might imagine about who I was or where I was going in that new jacket. I was buttoned up safe. The coat seemed like exactly the kind of prop I needed to tell myself a more convincing story. And a more convincing story seemed like exactly what I needed to better protect me. That coat was just one of the many, many stories in which I've tried to hide.

But even if you can get a story to work for a while, you'll still be afraid. And when it fails to meet the measure of life, as all stories do, you'll feel ashamed and your shame and guilt will manifest once again in that familiar pinch of disappointment.

Shame and guilt are life's way of protesting against the constriction of the too-tight story you're busy telling about it. The twist is that shame and guilt, manifest in this pinch, end up siding with your story and blaming life. Guilt doubles down on the self-important story you're telling about yourself. Guilt is sin seen from the perspective of your sinfulness. Even if you feel guilty about how you've hurt others, that guilt remains problematic because your guilt is about you and about how you didn't measure up to your story. Guilt recognizes your story's poor fit and then still demands that life measure up. It recognizes that your shoes are too small and too tight and then blames your feet for their size. Repentance is not about shaving down your toes, it's about taking off your shoes.

Jesus is not asking you to tell a better story or live your story more successfully, he's asking you to lose that story. "Those who find their life will lose it, and those who lose their life for my sake will find it" (Matthew 10:39 NRSV). Hell is when your story succeeds, not when it fails. Your suffocating story is the problem, not the solution. Surrender it and find your life. Your story is heavy and hard to bear. "Come to me," Jesus says, "all you that are weary and are carrying heavy burdens, and I will give you rest. Take my yoke upon you, and learn from me; for I am gentle and humble in heart, and you will find rest for your souls. For my yoke is easy, and my burden is light" (Matthew 11:28–30 NRSV). Put down the millstone of your story and take up the yoke of life instead. You will find Jesus' rest only in the work of caring for life. Let his life manifest itself in yours rather than trying to impose your story on the life he gives.

Obedience is important, but this isn't just about obedience. For sinners like us, the problem is not just that sin follows when we break the law. The problem is that sin severs God's law from life and then, rather than discarding it, cleverly repurposes it. In sin, the law, rather than rooting us in life, gets pressed into playing a leading role in the story you're trying to tell. Maybe in your story the law plays the role of an accuser: "You can't measure up, you're worthless!" Or, maybe in your story the law plays the role of an admirer: "You're so great, you keep the law, you do measure up!" But either way, reduced to the role of an extra in *your* story, the law kills you because it abets your preference for tidy stories over living bodies.

Keeping the law doesn't earn you heavenly merits and breaking the law doesn't earn you hellish demerits. Both merits and demerits are about you. The purpose of the law is to point you away from yourself, free you from the self-obsessed burden of your own story, and center you on Christ. You don't need to generate merit in order to be saved, you need instead to come unto Christ and "rely wholly upon the merits of him who is mighty to save" (2 Nephi 31:19). The law points wholly to Christ and his grace. Keeping the law is the work of relying on Christ's merit, not the work of generating your own. This is still hard work, but it is work of an entirely different kind.

When you sin, you sin not because you've failed to measure up to your story but because you've privileged your story in the first place. Privileging your story, you don't treat others or yourself with the care life requires. By freeing you from your story, Christ frees you from your guilt. He saves you by revealing that even your own life was never about you. Bought-back and story-poor, Christ frees space in your head to pay attention to someone other than yourself. You don't need rigid rules and expectations, you need Spirit. You need to be sensitive and responsive. Rather than filtering other people's

voices through the shame-making screen of your
story, you must learn to be responsible for the work
of caring for what you share with them.

Jesus doesn't want you to feel guilty, he wants you
to be responsible. Your stories aren't the truth, life
is. And only the truth can set you free.

Love,
A.

Faith

DEAR S.,

When your story wears thin and even you get tired of telling it, you'll need faith. This is not faith that in the end God will, against all odds, save your story. Just the opposite. This is faith that the life God offers you doesn't need your stories to dress it up. Dying is hard, but you can be reborn only when you trust God enough to let your stories die.

We often talk about faith as if people who don't have it are right about what it is. The fashionable line is that faith is a poor man's substitute for knowledge. When you lack good evidence and sound reason but you still want to say something is true, you need "faith." On this account, faith is a kind of admirably earnest wishful thinking about things that are lost, long past, or light-years away. And, on this account, spiritual progress is measured by your willful commitment to imposing on life a religious-sounding version of your story about how things should be. This account of faith is appealing to outsiders because it lets them box up religion as a curio.

But it's also often appealing to religious people because this version of faith doesn't press us to confess how deep sin goes. Faith, as an earnest brand of wishful thinking, works like an antacid to calm your stomach and help you keep your stories down. Saving faith, on the other hand, obliges you to just vomit them up.

Faith is not the same thing as common sense. It may be that, for you, God's reality is so natural and so consonant with common sense that you've never doubted it and don't have to work at believing in it. God is just given as part of how things are. This is true for many people. Believing in God isn't something they chose any more than they chose to believe that the sky is blue. They couldn't unchoose it if they tried. But this isn't enough. Though this common-sense acceptance of God's reality can be a blessing, it can also get in the way of practicing faith. It can lull you into thinking the hard work of being faithful is done when, in fact, you haven't even started.

On the other hand, it may be true that, for you, the existence of God is so unlikely and runs so counter to common sense that even an earnest kind of wishful thinking is more than you can credibly muster. God is just not given to you as part of how things are. This is also true for many people. Not believing just *is* and it's not something they chose or could magically unchoose. Though this common-sense godlessness can make things harder, it too can open a path to practicing faith. It may free you from common-sense idolatries.

Neither kind of common sense is faith. Moreover,

what seems like common sense—what seems so sensible because it's so conveniently complicit with your stories—should itself regularly come in for a healthy dose of skepticism. Either way, whether God is or isn't obvious to you, the work is the same: practice faithfully attending to the difficult, disturbing, and resistant truths God sets knocking at your door. Faith is a willingness, story or no, to care for what's right in front of you. Faith doesn't wish these difficult things away. It invites them in, breaks bread with them, and washes their feet. Faith is what you need to persist in truth as your sweet story, regardless of its content, gets overwritten by the real.

This is how Jesus said it would be. Don't look for God in the throne room. Don't look for him in outer space. You won't find him there. Jesus claims, instead, that he's hidden in plain sight. God constantly gives himself to us in the inconvenient, in the hungry, the outcast, the prisoner, the sinner. He gives himself in what we would like to ignore. "For I was hungry and you gave me food, I was thirsty and you gave me something to drink, I was a stranger and you welcomed me, I was naked and you gave me clothing, I was sick and you took care of me, I was in prison and you visited me." If we respond, incredulous: "Lord, when was it that we saw you hungry and gave you food, or thirsty and gave you something to drink?" He will respond that "just as you did it to one of the least of these . . . you did it to me" (Matthew 25:35–38, 40). Faith has to do with the least of these. It takes us down and into the unwieldy world, not up and away from it.

Faith is more like being faithful to your husband or wife than it is like believing in magic. Fidelity is the key. You may fall in love with someone because of how well they complement your story, but you'll prove yourself faithful to them only when you care more for the flawed, difficult, and unplotted life you end up sharing with them. Faith isn't the opposite of knowledge. Rather, like love, faith perfects knowledge by practicing fidelity to it.

Faith can't travel alone. It needs companions. As Paul says, "And now faith, hope, and love abide, these three; and the greatest of these is love" (1 Corinthians 13:13 NRSV). Faith serves charity, that pure love of Christ, by caring for the present and by anchoring hope in a world that already offers more than we're prepared to receive. Each of these three virtues tempers the others. Be faithful to what's given. Persist in attending to it until charity takes hold. Then forget what you'd planned and remember, instead, the joy of responding to what others need from you. Rather than hoping for satisfaction in the stories you tell about the next world, hope for charity in the hard work of caring for this one.

Or, as they say in Zen, waking up to life requires three things: great faith, great doubt, and great effort. Faith isn't a way of going to sleep. It's the work of waking up. And, in order to wake up, you'll need both great faith *and* great doubt. In itself, doubt is neither good nor bad. Its value depends on what you do with it. You can doubt what's real in order to stay asleep or you can doubt your daydreams in order to wake up. You can use doubt to protect you from the truth or you can use doubt to leave you vulnerable to it. You'll have doubts regardless. Repurpose them for the sake of faith. Saving doubt is a strong solvent that can burn holes in your stories and lead you back to the work of being faithful to life and, thus, to God. Practicing doubt for the sake of faith is hard work and it demands great effort. Great faith, great doubt, great effort.

When your faith falters and you're tempted to run, stand up and bear testimony instead. A testimony is a promise to stay. A testimony gives form to your great faith, it gives direction to your great doubt, and it publicly commits you to the great effort of trying to live what God gives. It is less a measure of your certainty about a list of facts than it is a mark of your commitment to bearing the truths that, despite their weakness, keep imposing themselves as a grace. In this way, bearing a testimony is like saying "I love you." A testimony doesn't just reflect what someone else has already decided, it is a declaration that, in the face of uncertainty, *you* have made a decision. Saying "I love you" or "I know the church is true" commits you to living in such a way as to *make* that love true.

Love,
A.

Scripture

Dear S.,

Get close to the scriptures. Do anything you can. God is in there. Moses told his people to put bits of scripture in little boxes and, when praying, to tie one box to their arm and the other to their head. Strap the bible to your forehead. Wear the Book of Mormon on your sleeve. Sleep with your scriptures under your pillow. Tape Pharisees to your bathroom mirror. Underline everything. Pack your margins with notes. Read Paul out loud like poetry. Copy the Book of Mormon by hand. Read the bible backwards one verse at a time. Tally their letters like numbers. Squeeze their verses like oranges. Know Isaiah by heart. Love Matthew like a brother. Sing the psalms as your prayers. Read them in Hebrew. Read them in Greek. Read them in Russian and Spanish and Japanese. Translate them all into English and then back again. Do like the Lord told Ezekiel: "'Son of man, eat this scroll I am giving you and fill your stomach with it.' So I ate it, and it tasted as sweet as honey in my mouth" (Ezekiel 3:3 NIV). Don't just read the scriptures, eat them. Get them not only into your head but down into your gut.

The restoration restored scripture. God showed himself to Joseph Smith first as flesh and bone and then as ink on paper. When he appeared in the sacred grove, Jesus quoted scripture. When he appeared in Joseph's bedroom, Moroni quoted scripture and then sent Joseph to unearth more. Joseph translated the Book of Mormon. And then he retranslated the bible. And then he revealed the Book of Abraham. Then Joseph went back and started again. He never stopped working on his translation of the bible. Brigham Young even seemed to suggest that, if Joseph were still alive, he might try a fresh translation of the Book of Mormon.

Joseph always expected more revelations, and "translation" was one vital name for the hard work of receiving them. For Joseph, translation was less a chore to be done than a way, day by day, of holding life open for God's word. Translating scripture is a way of renewing life. In translation we lend our lives—our minds, our ears, our mouths—to the local resurrection of old texts, dead words, and lost voices. We put down our stories and take up theirs. And as we give voice to them, they, for a time, rejoin us in the land of the living.

Joseph produced, as God required, the first public translations of the scriptures we now share. But that work, open-ended all along, is unfinished. Now, the task is ours. When you read the scriptures, don't just lay your eyes like stones on the pages. Roll up your sleeves and translate them again. Every morning and every night, we are each commanded to sit down at our kitchen tables, spread out our books and notes and papers and pens, and, with a prayer in hand, finish what Joseph started. It is not enough for Nephi to have translated Isaiah into reformed Egyptian or for Joseph to have translated Nephi into King James English. You and I must translate these books again. Word by word, line by line, verse by verse, chapter by chapter, God wants the whole thing translated once more, and this time he wants it translated into your native tongue, inflected by your native concerns, and written in your native flesh. To be a Mormon is to do once more, on your own small scale, the same kind of work that Joseph did.

To succeed, you'll have to pray always. You'll have to study it out in your mind. You'll have to listen to the beating of your heart. You'll have to consult the best books. You'll have to take careful notes. And then you'll have to bring all these raw ingredients to bear on how God wants you to retranslate the next verse you'll read. Led by word and Spirit, you'll be empowered to do it and when you're done, you must ask the Lord if—for you, at this time, at this place— you've done it right.

You'll know you've done it right if, as a result of the work, you repent. "Say nothing but repentance unto this generation," the Lord told Oliver Cowdery when he came to help Joseph translate the Book of Mormon (D&C 6:9). This is your charge too: translate nothing but repentance. When you're reading them right, the scriptures will bring you up short. They'll call you into question. They'll challenge your stories and deflate your pretensions. They'll show you how you've been wrong and they'll show you how to make things right.

You'll need faith to undertake these translations as acts of repentance. You'll have to trust that the books can withstand your scrutiny and you'll have to trust that God, despite their antiquity, can be contemporary in them. The Lord counseled Joseph that, "as all have not faith, seek ye diligently and teach one another words of wisdom; yea, seek out of the best books words of wisdom; seek learning even by study and also by faith" (D&C 88:118). This is good, though circuitous, advice. On one hand, if you lack faith, seek wisdom out of the best books. On the other hand, if you lack wisdom, seek learning by faith. Your ability to translate with power will depend on your faith and it will be amplified by your familiarity with the world's best books. The wider you read in Laozi, Shakespeare, Austen, Dogen, Plato, Dante, Krishna, Sappho, Goethe, Confucius, Tolstoy, and Homer, the better off you'll be. The more familiar you are with Israelite histories, Near Eastern archaeologies, and secular biblical scholarship, the richer your translations will be rendered. Don't be afraid for scripture and don't be afraid of these other books. Claim it all as your own. Doubtless, the world's best books have their flaws, but this just means that they too must be translated. You'll need to translate *them* so that they can contribute to your own translations. As long as these other books help you to translate repentance, then you're still doing it right.

Don't balk at this responsibility or hand it off to church leaders. Our minds go dark and our hearts go cold when we set this work aside. "Your minds in times past have been darkened," the Lord told Joseph, "because of unbelief, and because you have treated lightly the things you have received—which vanity and unbelief have brought the whole church under condemnation" (D&C 84:54–55). Our minds go dark because we've treated this responsibility lightly. We don't sit down with the scriptures and we don't study them out in our minds. And, to our discredit, we've often dismissed the world's best books rather than translate them. As a result, we'll "remain under this condemnation" until we "repent and remember the new covenant, even the Book of Mormon" (D&C 84:57).

The Book of Mormon is this new covenant. It is itself what God promises you. It is given to you as a Urim and Thummim, as your own personal seer stone. Look into it and learn how to see the world by its light. And as you do, you'll be shown not only how to say but to *do* what the Lord requires.

Love,
A.

Prayer

Dear S.,

When you pray, the most important thing is to stay awake. To pray, you'll need time, you'll need a private place—a room, a closet, a porch—and you'll need silence. Avoid praying in your bed or at your bedside. If you want to sit in a chair, hard chairs are better than soft ones. If you want to kneel or sit on the floor, keep your back straight. Speaking out loud, even in a whisper, can help you stay on track. Leaving your eyes open, though unfocused, can also help. Experiment. The rule is: do whatever keeps you praying instead of sleeping.

When you pray, notice how the same thing happens almost every time. You address God and then you start to think about what you should say and then this prompts you to think about something else and then, caught up in thinking about this other thing, you forget that you were saying a prayer. Your brain browns out. Eventually, after a few minutes, you remember why you were kneeling there in the first place. This moment is the key. When, for the first time, you remember this, your prayer can start for real.

Don't be discouraged. The substance of a prayer is this willingness to remember, to heave your wandering mind back, once more, in the direction of God, and then, when it drifts off yet again, to heave it still another time. To pray is to practice remembering God. The more frequently you forget, the more chances you'll have to remember, and the more you remember, the deeper your prayer will go. With patience and practice, you'll remember God more often. Soon, instead of forgetting God for whole minutes at a time, you'll remember him every half-minute or so. When you get that far, keep going! As your prayers gather momentum and that frequency increases, your connection to God will not just spark but burn. And when that happens, the lights will come on. And you'll wake up.

In prayer, you can practice remembering God in one of two ways. You can practice by remembering what you were saying or you can practice by remembering to listen. The first way is important, the second way is imperative.

In the first case, you might try asking God for help with specific problems you have. This is good. Or, better, you might try asking God to help you help someone else with a specific problem. Or, also excellent, you might try expressing gratitude. For the most part, the more specific you can be and the less your prayers are about you, the better they'll be. Prayer deepens as it moves from self-concern to service to gratitude.

But talking is just half a prayer. As a rule of thumb, take however much time you spend talking and then devote at least as much to listening. Listening, though, is harder. Without the thread of a particular concern to guide you, you'll be especially prone to forget. To keep your attention steady, you might go for a walk and, to calm your mind, pay attention to the feel of each footstep. Or you might stay still and pay attention to your breath. In this case, be still and breathe naturally. Feel your lungs slowly expand and contract. Notice how the air is cold when you draw it in through your nose but warm when your body presses it back out. Let everything settle. Then, against the backdrop of this stillness, note what feelings you have and what impressions come. Don't get carried away by these thoughts or feelings, but sit with them. When you're done, try to act directly on your impressions and try to carry your prayerful stillness into the rest of your day.

In all of this, try to pray like Jesus. In his final hours, Jesus modeled two kinds of prayer. In the Garden of Gethsemane, on the eve of his crucifixion, Jesus withdrew from his disciples. Alone, he "fell on his face, and prayed, saying, O my Father, if it be possible, let this cup pass from me: nevertheless not as I will, but as thou wilt" (Matthew 26:39). In all our prayers we must, in the end, do as Jesus does here. We may express our will to God but then, in silence, we must submit that will to his. Our willingness to wait on the Lord in silence and listen for his voice is what proves the truth of our continual confession: not as I will, but as thou wilt. Not my story but thine. On Luke's account, after Jesus offered this prayer, "there appeared an angel unto him from heaven, strengthening him" (Luke 22:43). You will find strength in prayer as you submit your will to God's and as your willingness to listen makes God's voice audible.

This first prayer, though difficult, is encouraging. The second is more harrowing. The next day, nailed to the cross and mocked by scribes and thieves, darkness shrouded the earth. In this darkness, "about the ninth hour Jesus cried with a loud voice, saying, Eli, Eli, lama sabachthani? that is to say, My God, my God, why hast thou forsaken me?" (Matthew 27:46). This, too, is a prayer. It is a prayer that arises from an unbroken willingness to wait on the Lord in silence. Sometimes when you pray and wait in silence, a messenger will come, you'll hear the voice of the Lord, and you'll be empowered to do as God directs. But sometimes when you pray and wait in silence, there will only be silence and you will wonder where God has gone. When this happens, you'll have to make a choice. You'll have to decide whether to get up and leave the room or whether to continue in silence. If you choose the first, then you'll return to the bustle of the world. But if you persist in the second, you may discover something more powerful and primal than the voice of the Lord. You may discover that God's silence is not itself a rebuke but an invitation. The heavens aren't empty, they're quiet. And God, rather than turning you away, may be inviting you to share this silence with him. This is part of what atonement looks like: sitting in shared silence with God.

I once sat in silence for ten days. I sat in an old room on the floor. For seven days, I practiced prayer. I would forget and then remember and then forget again. Sometimes I would forget for hours at a time. Sometimes I would remember for more. On the eighth day, my mind was wild and my heart was restless. I wanted to get up and leave. But I sat. Then, while in that room, sitting on that floor, my heart broke. And I wept silent tears. And I woke up. The summer sun was full in the window and the air was warm. "Be still," the Lord says, "and know that I am God" (Psalm 46:10).

Don't forget to pray.

Love,
A.

History

DEAR S.,

It's easy to think that things are worse than they used to be. People have thought this for thousands of years. It's not hard to see why. While today's troubles are so pressing, we have only pale memories of what they suffered yesterday.

Nephi thought this. In Helaman 7, Nephi has just returned from an unsuccessful mission to his fellow Nephites. Retiring to his garden tower to pray, he cries out to God in despair:

> Oh, that I could have had my days in the
> days when my father Nephi first came out
> of the land of Jerusalem, that I could have
> joyed with him in the promised land; then
> were his people easy to be entreated, firm
> to keep the commandments of God, and
> slow to be led to do iniquity; and they
> were quick to hearken unto the words of
> the Lord—Yea, if my days could have been
> in those days, then would my soul have

had joy in the righteousness of my
brethren. But behold, I am consigned that
these are my days, and that my soul shall
be filled with sorrow because of this the
wickedness of my brethren. (Helaman
7:7–9)

Crushed by the hardness of his people's hearts,
Nephi calls out to God. Then, in a move that is
acutely human, he laments living in a day when
men are fallen and faithless. The golden age when
people "were easy to be entreated, firm to keep the
commandments of God, and slow to be led to do in-
iquity" has long passed and our present world is a
mess.

Nephi's anguish for his people is genuine but his
version of Nephite history is strained. Were things
really any different for the original Nephi? Were they
easier? It doesn't look that way. We might as easily
imagine this wail for a lost golden age coming out of
that first Nephi's mouth as anyone's. Remember a
condemned Jerusalem? A desperate flight into the
wilderness? Laman and Lemuel?

Even having safely arrived in the promised land,
Lehi's family is barely settled before, Nephi says,
"the Lord did warn me, that I, Nephi, should depart
from them"—*them* being half of his own family,
some of whom wanted to murder him—"and flee
into the wilderness" (2 Nephi 5:5). From there, the
situation is fragile enough that, as soon as Nephi
himself dies, Jacob fears the whole thing is headed
over a cliff. "The people of Nephi," Jacob writes,

"under the reign of the second king, began to grow hard in their hearts, and indulge themselves somewhat in wicked practices, such as like unto David of old desiring many wives and concubines, and also Solomon, his son. Yea, and they also began to search much gold and silver, and began to be lifted up somewhat in their pride" (Jacob 1:15–16).

Nephi's small band of refugees may have lived, at least for a time, "after the manner of happiness," but we have no reason to doubt that these people suffered from the same stubbornness, weakness, and vanity that weighs on us all (2 Nephi 5:27). Even of himself, Nephi says: "O wretched man that I am! Yea, my heart sorroweth because of my flesh; my soul grieveth because of mine iniquities. I am encompassed about, because of the temptations and the sins which do so easily beset me. And when I desire to rejoice, my heart groaneth because of my sins" (2 Nephi 4:17–19).

Annie Dillard's account of how we tend to romanticize flannel-board versions of biblical people gets this just right. In *Holy the Firm*, Dillard says:

> A blur of romance clings to our notions of "publicans," "sinners," "the poor," "the people in the marketplace," "our neighbors," as though of course God should reveal himself, if at all, to these simple people, these Sunday school watercolor figures, who are so purely themselves in their tattered robes, who are single in themselves, while we now are various, complex, and full at heart. We are busy.

So, I see now, were they. Who shall ascend
into the hill of the Lord? or who shall
stand in his holy place? There is no one
but us. There is no one to send, nor a
clean hand, nor a pure heart on the face of
the earth, nor in the earth, but only us, a
generation comforting ourselves with the
notion that we have come at an awkward
time, that our innocent fathers are all
dead—as if innocence had ever been—
and our children busy and troubled, and
we ourselves unfit, not yet ready, having
each of us chosen wrongly, made a false
start, failed, yielded to impulse and the
tangled comfort of pleasures, and grown
exhausted, unable to seek the thread,
weak, and involved. But there is no one
but us. There has never been.

Who will ascend the hill of the Lord? There is no
one to send but us. There never has been.

There is a kind of false comfort in consoling ourselves with the idea that, while our days are evil, the
world once was good. This modest comfort slips easily into excuse or recrimination. On the one hand,
we excuse ourselves from giving all that God de-
manded of previous generations because, unlike our
quasi-angelic ancestors, we are mere mortals, dis-
tracted and fragile and weak. "Good for them!" we
may shout, eagerly cheering their distant greatness
as a way of justifying our present stupor. On the
other hand, we might use these stories of a golden

age as a sword rather than a shield. We might set to work scrupulously indicting ourselves and others for not being quasi-angelic and larger than life (like they were) and punish ourselves for being, instead, the hungry mortals that we are. There are saving and damning differences between lives, but these variations apply to different ways of being cracked and hungry. They aren't differences in kind.

This is both the good news and the bad news. While it is scary to think that God works through weak, partial, and limited mortals like us, the only thing scarier would be thinking that he doesn't.

This rule applies to our own church history as much as it does to stories from places long ago and far away. It's a false dilemma to claim that either God works through practically flawless people or God doesn't work at all. The gospel isn't a celebration of God's power to work with flawless people. The gospel is a celebration of God's willingness to work today, in our world, in our lives, with people who clearly aren't. To demand that church leaders, past and present, show us only a mask of angelic pseudo-perfection is to deny the gospel's most basic claim: that God's grace works through our weakness. We need prophets, not idols. Our prophets and leaders will not turn out to be who you want them to be. They are not, in fact, even what God might want them to be. But they are real and God really can, nonetheless, work through their imperfections to extend his perfect love.

Our church manuals and church histories are sometimes shy about this good news. With good intentions, they worry over your faith. Sometimes they seem too much like that friend of a friend who really just wants you to *like* them, and so they pretend to only like the same vanilla things they think you do. But God is stronger stuff than this. And the scriptures certainly are as well. If, as the bible makes clear, God can work through liars, thieves, adulterers, murderers, prostitutes, tax collectors, and beggars, he can certainly work around (or even through) Joseph Smith's clandestine practice of polygamy, Brigham Young's strong-armed experiments in theocracy, or George Albert Smith's mental illness.

In the parable of the mustard seed, Jesus innocently compared the kingdom of God to "a mustard seed that someone took and sowed in the garden; it grew and became a tree; and the birds of the air made nests in its branches" (Luke 13:19 NRSV). This is a nice story, but we've forgotten about mustard seeds. It would have been plain to Jesus' audience that this parable was meant to vex them. People have big ideas about what the kingdom of God is supposed to be like, but teeny tiny mustard seeds like Jesus described don't grow into towering cedars. Generally, they don't amount to much more than overgrown bushes. More, Jesus' audience would have known that mustard plants aren't typically grown in gardens. When growing a garden, you're more likely to spend your time weeding them out. Rather than being a cash crop, mustard plants are more like stubborn weeds liable to hijack your whole plot. Jesus means this parable as a kind of warning. Don't expect, Jesus says, the kingdom of God to look like a massive oak tree. Expect it to be more like a weed that, without your quite intending it, overruns your garden and crowds out the stories you'd been hoping to tell.

At some point, God will ask you to sacrifice on his altar not only your stories about your own life but your versions of *his* stories as well. Your softly lit watercolor felt-board versions of scripture stories and church history must, like all your stories, be abandoned at his feet, and the messy, vibrant, and inconvenient truths that characterize God's real work with real people will have to take center stage. If they don't, then how will God's work in your hungry, messy, and inconvenient life ever do the same?

When God knocks, don't creep up to the door and look through the peephole to see if he looks like you thought he would. Rush to the door and throw it open.

Love,
A.

Science

Dear S.,

The world is big and it's hard to find a handle. Problems of scale abound. On a human scale, the world looks flat, a hundred years seems like a long time, and the sun pretty obviously circles the earth. Just look up in the sky. Every morning you can watch with your own eyes as the sun circles back above us, and every evening you can watch it circle back below. But the world is much rounder, time much deeper, and the earth more eccentric than this. We see the world through only the narrowest of keyholes. Given these limits, we can depend on getting things wrong, and we should welcome God's rolling revelation that the world is much, much stranger than it seems.

God has been rushing to show us more of this strange world. You name it: fossils, black holes, x-rays, DNA, set theory, one-dimensional strings, Neanderthals, dark matter, brain imaging, big data, evolution, retroviruses, interplanetary travel, the Higgs boson, non-euclidean geometries, Mars rovers, etc. God used to send us an occasional rain. Now the revelations come as a flood. We live in a postdiluvian world, and the rain falls harder every day.

God anticipated this downpour. "Teach ye diligently and my grace shall attend you," the Lord tells Joseph Smith, "that you may be instructed more perfectly in theory, in principle, in doctrine, in the law of the gospel, in all things that pertain to the kingdom of God, that are expedient for you to understand" (D&C 88:78). This attendant grace is expansive. It touches not just the principles, doctrines, and laws of the gospel, but "all things" that are expedient. This includes "things both in heaven and in the earth, and under the earth, things which have been, things which are, things which must shortly come to pass" (D&C 88:79). As we watch from our sofas, the world's secrets are getting shouted from the rooftops, its fossils are being turned out of their graves, its cored icebergs are testifying to God's long-suffering care, and the voice of Mitochondrial Eve is speaking to us from the dust. Despite our self-absorption, willful ignorance, and pet parochialisms, God is prying open our eyes and ears. Who has ears to hear? God speaks both scripture and science. Listen for his voice.

As a rule, God works with whatever small knowledge of the world we've already got. He speaks to people "in their weakness, after the manner of their language, that they might come to understanding" (D&C 1:24). Our sacred texts witness God's willingness to suffer this weakness. They tell a mix of stories from many different times and places that illustrate what happens when the strength of God's polyphonic voice gets funneled into the weakness of our mono-channel ears. It is tempting to ignore the inconsistencies that result and impose on our scriptures a false uniformity, but we should hold off. These books are worth more rough. Uncut, they bear witness to real revelations given to real people, because they also bear witness to the host of real weaknesses that helped socket God's word into their worlds.

Take Genesis 1 as an example. The Hebrews, as was common for their time and place, thought the world was basically a giant snow globe. When God wanted to reveal his hand in the creation of their world, he borrowed and repurposed the common-sense cosmology they already had. He wasn't worried about its inaccuracies, he was worried about showing *his* hand at work in shaping their world as *they* knew it.

In the beginning, there was only a kind of watery confusion. Then God divided the light from the dark. He divided the waters above from the waters below by inserting an immense sheet of hammered tin whose arc could form the bubble that is our sky. He set sun, moon, and stars spinning in their tracks through the world's roof and then built heaven on top of it. Sometimes this roof leaks, water trickles through, and it rains. Sometimes the heavens are tight as a drum. Then God raised some dry ground in the center of this dome, marked Jerusalem as the world's belly button, and set plants growing. Once the plants were planted, he filled the earth with all the kinds of animals that Noah would later need to squeeze aboard his ark. To round the whole thing out, God made men and women in his own indelible image. Then, though there was much more he could have said or corrected, God called this world good. And in that light, the Hebrews could see its goodness better too.

I believe in a literal reading of this text. I believe the Hebrews literally thought the world was like that, and I believe that God literally ran with it and revealed his grace at work in their lives through it. More, I believe that God is just as literally showing himself to us in and through that continually rolling revelation that is science as we know it. The world given to us is not the same as the world given to them. We have two worlds here. But though our worlds diverge, it is the same God peeping through. Believing that the God of their world is just as surely the God of ours doesn't commit us to believing in their version of the world. Rather, it commits us to believing in a God whose grace is full enough to fill them both.

I didn't used to think this. Fresh from my mission, I was full of a zealous simplicity that would not truck with more than one world. There is a virtue to that simplicity, but there is a price too. In the end, the price seemed to me too high and the return too small. The world wanted to be bigger than I was letting it, stranger than I wanted it, and darker than I was willing to abide. The world wanted to be many. It wanted to be worlds without end. My wife, herself a biologist, bore with my plagiarized anti-science screeds. "Biological evolution on a scale of

3.5 billion years can't be made to fit that biblical world," I argued. And there is something to this argument. In fact, I still think it holds. But now I think it's the wrong question. The question isn't: can evolution be made to fit with the biblical idea of the *world*? The question is: can evolution be made to fit with the biblical *God* who showed himself in that biblical world? I don't have any revelatory answers about how they fit, but given that both God and evolution are real, I assume the answer is yes. They do fit. Now it's up to us to open our doors, zip our slickers, and step out into the storm of revelations raining down on us. It's up to us to keep thinking and praying and testing from here.

This is hard and often uncomfortable work. But it's good for us. It's good for us, in general, to own up to the prickly aspects of our history. And, in this sense, a willingness to own our deep biological past may be just as vital to our future as a willingness to own our seer stones, racism, and polygamy. Recent or distant, locked in vaults or bones, history is history. We can't afford to play games whitewashing Brigham Young or Homo erectus.

For my part, I'm convinced that the tested revelations that now shape our shared understanding of the world—that history slides on a line that is billions rather than thousands of years long, that our world lies on the periphery of worlds without number, that space is unthinkably blind and deep, and that life slowly and painfully emerged in our world as the joint product of terrible necessities and blessed accidents—I'm convinced that these revelations are among the most commanding God has ever given.

God told his prophets all along that a savior would come in the meridian of time, but until recently we had no idea how much time he would need to save. The length of time's fraught and wandering line was a revelation sealed, like a book, in the rocks beneath our feet. These rocks have finally broken their silence, and, in light of what they're saying, we know now that God's saving grace must be even more cunning and enduring than we've yet had strength to imagine.

Love,
A.

Hunger

Dear S.,

I can see that you're hungry. And, though you may doubt it, this hunger is a grace, something you can neither command nor deserve but that, nonetheless, is given. This, too, is how a body is. Your body is a gift, and to be alive in your body is to live with this hunger.

When Jesus was baptized, he, like you, began a new life. The heavens opened for him, God spoke to him, and the Spirit filled him. "Jesus, full of the Holy Spirit, returned from the Jordan and was led by the Spirit in the wilderness, where for forty days he was tempted by the devil. He ate nothing at all during those days, and when they were over, he was famished" (Luke 4:1–2 NRSV). Newborn and Spirit-led, the first thing revealed to Jesus is hunger. Immediately after God speaks, the Spirit "drives him out into the wilderness" and acquaints him with a thirst and fatigue forty days in the making (compare Mark 1:12). Jesus cannot be the life of the world if he does not, in his bones, understand the wild hunger that propels it.

If religion is about living life rather than dodging it, then this hunger can't just be brushed aside, tamped down, or covered over. Your heart beats and your lungs expand and your brain thinks and your cells divide because of it. Like the ocean tide, the push and pull of your body's needs give order and direction to your day. They put you in bed at night and pull you back out in the morning. They set your table for breakfast, lunch, and dinner. They stand you in the shower. They wrap you in warm clothing. Soliciting you, these hungers give body to your most elemental joys.

Your hungers are trying to teach you what it means to be a body. Bodies are organs of passing. Bodies channel what they can of the world through your narrow walls of flesh and bone. Bodies pass light through your eyes, sounds through your ears, smells through your nose, tastes through your tongue, food through your bowels, air through your lungs, blood through your veins, electricity through your nerves. These things all come and these things all go. None of them stay. Your body borrows its living from the world. Satisfactions always wane and your hungers are a sign of their passing. More, these hungers don't just mark the passing of what has, for a time, sustained you. They mark the passing of the body that you are.

Never forget this: you are hungry because you are dying. That is the kind of thing a body is. We live our mortal lives mortally wounded by a hunger that will not quit. The story of your life will be the story of how you choose to live with and through this fact.

For the sake of life, you must greet this hunger as Jesus did, with the kind of care, patience, and attention enabled by Spirit.

Gnawed by hungers, you'll be tempted to make one of two mistakes. Aware of life's restless difficulty, you'll be tempted to try to "solve" the problem of your hunger by (1) satisfying it, or (2) purging it. Neither will work and both amount to a rejection of life. Trying to avoid the hunger that animates life either by satisfying it or by purging it, you'll only end up avoiding life itself. Rather than being alive, you'll discover that you've strategized yourself into being plain undead. This zombie-like disconnection from life's hunger—and, thus, God's presence—is called sin or spiritual death.

Don't run from your hunger. Don't call it names, curse it, regret it, or shame yourself with it. But don't indulge it either. Rather, *care* for your hunger. Pay attention. Watch it grow and fade. Become acquainted with and sensitive to it. Hunger marks your openness to the world, your dependence on it, your vulnerability to it. Your hunger is an "X" that marks that all-important spot where your life and the world's substance overlap. This open vulnerability to people and food and air is not a curse but a gift. Welcome the world, love it, and express trust in it by caring about your hunger for it.

Learn to note all the little, deadening tactics you use to keep life at arm's length. Learn, instead, to draw life close. Our lives are short and so much of them is spent eating and sleeping. We have to get this part right. Learn to eat with gratitude and care.

Eat like you would like to eat again. Save some hunger for later. Eat what makes you feel good, not just while you're chewing it but two hours later. Learn to go to bed early and get up early. Don't cling to the day or the night by staying up too late or sleeping in too long. Sleep like you would like to sleep again.

See the truth about sin and the spiritual death that sin causes. Your spiritual life will pivot around your first-person full-bodied discovery that sin is a gesture of self-defense. Sin is a way of recoiling in fear from life's vulnerability. The spiritual death you suffer is a wall that *you* built between yourself and your own life in order to protect yourself from it. An abundant life depends on trusting the Spirit and letting this wall fall.

Living the gospel means learning how to live. It means learning to eat and sleep. Plant yourself in your hunger and let your life grow out of it. Let God grow in you. Hear his voice in your need. Let Jesus resurrect you right now, in this life, even before you're done dying. Let him put your spirit back in your hungry body.

Love,
A.

Sex

Dear S.,

Soon, you'll be hungry not only to renew life but to
make it. A hunger for sex will grow in you that is
just as real, just as native, and just as pressing as
your need for food and sleep. Remember that your
hunger for intimacy, like all hungers, is a grace not a
punishment.

This new hunger is different from the others.
You'll die if you don't eat and breathe, but you won't
die if you don't have sex—though, to be honest, you
may sometimes feel like you will. This new hunger
is different because it is not just a hunger for food or
air but for another *person,* and that person's needs
and feelings and fears are just as real and just as
complicated as your own. And there is something
else to always bear in mind. The intimacy you crave
now not only involves your responsibility to care for
the needs of another person, it involves your responsibility to care for the fact that this intimacy can
make a new person. Sex gives life.

This hunger for intimacy is like an ocean. It will

come like a flood and you will feel lost at sea. When you were a child, you walked on dry ground. In order to become an adult, you'll have to learn how to swim. You are no more responsible for being at sea than you are for needing to breathe. And, though some may say different, you are not guilty because the ocean is wet. You did not choose this hunger, you did not choose your gender, and you did not choose its orientation. But, however the particulars may vary, the task remains basically the same: learn how to care for this hunger. Caring for this hunger will take practice and patience. Be kind to yourself as you stumble through.

In church, we say: learn to be chaste. This is right, but we have to be clear. Chastity, as a way of practicing care, doesn't purge or deny this hunger. You are chaste when you are full of life, and you are full of life when you are faithful to the hungers that root it.

To care for this hunger, you must do just as you did with the others. You cannot get rid of your hunger either by pandering to it or by purging it. Both strategies deny hunger and leave you undead. Church-talk about sexual purity is meant to keep you close to life and warn you against trying to end your hunger by carelessly indulging it. But while talk of purity may help constrain your hunger, it can also conspire with the impulse to purge it. And trying to get rid of your hunger by purging it, even for the sake of purity, will just as surely leave you spiritually dead as indulging it. The measure of chastity is life, and life, by divine design, is messy. If used without care, aiming for purity is as likely to maim you as save you. Don't became a slave *to* your hunger and don't try to make a slave *of* your hunger. Slavery is sin, and sin is death.

The way is clear even if it's not easy. Commit to respecting the bodies of other people and commit to caring for your own. When it comes to bodies that are not your own, the line is bright: don't use pornography and don't have sex outside of marriage. Inevitably, you'll be exposed to pornography but don't use it. Pornography trades your hunger for cash. It doesn't care for you, and it destroys the lives of the men and women it uses to lure you. Don't be complicit in this catastrophe. In general, don't date seriously before you are old enough to be serious. Keep your hands to yourself. Wait to kiss and then kiss like you would like to kiss again tomorrow, not like you want to get all the kissing done, once and for all, today.

Be patient with your affections. I kissed a girl for the first time when I was fourteen. She was sixteen. She had brown eyes and dark hair. I was surprised by her. When we kissed, I crossed a mild but important line—you only get one first kiss—and I didn't really want to cross it. It was winter, after school, after a basketball game, and we were waiting outside. It was dark and snowing and we were alone. She asked me to kiss her. I shuffled my feet and made excuses. She asked me again and I said okay. So she took my hand, leaned in, and kissed me. It was sweet. I'll never forget it. But still I was uneasy. I knew I hadn't kissed her because I loved her or because I was starved for a physical connection—though I did care about her and I was hungry. The truth is that I was afraid to kiss her, and, in the end, I only kissed her *because* I was afraid. I was afraid not to do what she wanted. I was fourteen, I was awkward, I had bad skin, I didn't have many close friends, and I needed her to stay close by. Watch for this unsteady mix of hunger and need and fear. Don't use the forms of love to win acceptance and paper over your fears. Take courage from love and do what's best.

With respect to your own body, you must practice. You must be patient with its immaturity because you are still growing. And you must have compassion for its weakness because you are still mortal. Learning to be chaste is like learning to play the piano. There is only one way to learn: you must practice the music without already knowing how to play. Similarly, you must care for your hunger without already knowing its strength, its character, or how to direct it. You have no choice but to learn as you go. Life has never before been lived in your body.

Chastity is not a kind of perfection. You may have arrived in this world innocent, but chastity is something more. Chastity is not something you are born with and then break or lose, it is something that is made. It is something that must, with years of patient and compassionate effort, be cultivated and grown and gathered and sealed.

Caring for your own hunger will teach you how to care for the body of the person you'll one day love. Watch your hunger closely. See how, like the ocean, it has a rhythm, tides that come in and out, and waves that break. See how it gets tangled with the stories you tell yourself and with the fantasies you entertain. See how it gets knotted together with all kinds of hopes and shames and fears. Notice how, when the tide of your hunger goes out, this doesn't suddenly mean you're chaste. And notice how, when the tide comes in, this doesn't suddenly mean that you aren't.

Listen, practice prayer, and let your hunger teach you. When you are alone and feel, as you often will, a growing hunger for sex, don't always run away. Don't automatically distract yourself from it or automatically lose yourself in it. Rather, try doing the one thing we're often most afraid to do: pay direct attention to the hunger itself. Just watch. Acknowledge the hunger's weight, autonomy, and reality. Notice that there is a difference between the images, fears, and fantasies that fuel the hunger and the physical sensations proper to the hunger itself. Then, instead of paying attention to the fantasies that stoke it, pay attention to the physical sensations that compose it. Become friends with them and watch patiently as their grip loosens. Don't pour fuel on the fire by entertaining your fantasies, but don't try to put out the fire either. Just watch the flames as they burn, on their own, back down to coals. Practicing chastity means caring for these coals. Practicing chastity means learning how to offer this hunger back to God as a prayer.

You'll do a better job listening on some days than others. You'll have ups and downs. The impulse to explore your own body when you are young and alone isn't evil, but it does need the kind of tempering that only experience, practice, and maturity can engrain. Don't panic when, as a teenager, you discover that you don't yet have experience or maturity.

Most importantly, even when you feel you've done wrong, your job is still the same: practice caring for your life as it's actually given rather than fretting guiltily over how you imagine it should be. Shame and fear will not help you here. Satan, not Jesus, is the accuser. When you experience fear or shame or guilt, your job is to practice care for them as well. Don't hurt yourself with them. Let the fear and guilt come, let them go, and learn what they too have to teach about the root of life.

Ask for help. You're not alone. You don't have to manage this by yourself. Talk to your parents. Let them talk to you. It's hard to believe, but *everyone* feels what you feel.

I pray you'll find someone to whom you can seal yourself and to whom you can promise your hunger. And I pray that, if your circumstances are more complex, God will show you how best to care for your life in light of them.

Love,
A.

Temples

DEAR S.,

My mom and dad were married in 1966. To make
ends meet, my dad joined the navy. While he was at
sea, missionaries knocked on my mother's door. "I
think my husband's a Mormon," she said. My dad
came home and he was surprised. My older brother
was born in 1969 and my older sister in 1971. They
went to church together. In 1973, they packed themselves and a cooler full of bologna sandwiches into a
car that I wouldn't trust for trips to the grocery store
and drove two thousand miles from Pennsylvania to
Salt Lake City. They were all four sealed in the Salt
Lake Temple that May. Then, marshaling nickels and
dimes, they made the long drive home. When I was
born two years later, I came stamped and sealed, already bound by promises I hadn't been present to
make and already overwritten with names and bless-
ings I had in no way earned. My little sister, born
two years after that, came bundled the same way.

From the start, these powers and prayers and
priesthoods were at work in my life. And from the

start, they were preparing me for one thing: to see the face of God.

Two priesthoods were revealed to Joseph Smith, a lesser and a greater. While the lesser is preparatory, the greater "administereth the gospel and holdeth the key of the mysteries of the kingdom, even the key of the knowledge of God. Therefore, in the ordinances thereof, the power of godliness is manifest. And without the ordinances thereof, and the authority of the priesthood, the power of godliness is not manifest unto men in the flesh; for without this no man can see the face of God, even the Father, and live" (D&C 84:19–22). As Mormons, we rightly place great emphasis on our rituals. Baptisms, sacraments, ordinations, washings, anointings, endowments, sealings: our ordinances give order to our desires and they clear space in our lives for the mysteries of the kingdom. We return to them again and again because they are keys to the mysteries and because God's power is manifest there. These ordinances have the power to open and close. They are doors that open a way out, doors that usher us into unfamiliar places, and doors that close behind us. You'll know an ordinance worked when, having passed through its door, you're no longer sure where you are.

This is especially true with the temple. Our baptisms, sacraments, and ordinations are public, but our washings, anointings, endowments, and sealings are not. These are attended instead by a compelling privacy. The temple is a place apart. In the stillness of the temple, we wear white pants and dresses, white robes and sashes, white caps and veils. In the temple, God prepares us to be endowed with faith and sealed in love by washing our arms and hands and heads, by anointing us with oil, and by giving us new clothes. In the temple, we're given an endowment. An endowment is a gift. God gives this gift in the form of a long story about the creation of the world, about Adam and Eve, about evil and suffering, about promises and sacrifices, and about what we must do to pass back through the veil and see God's face. In the temple, we imagine what it would be like to be Adam and Eve. We sit for an hour and watch and listen and imagine what it would be like to make the promises they made, to accept the symbols God entrusted to their care, and to receive the graces that followed. And then we are invited to do as they did. Finally, in the temple, brides and grooms kneel at altars and clasp hands as a sealer ratifies their marriage with God's own binding seal. And once we've passed through these veils for ourselves, we do all this again (and again) for our dead.

The work we do in the temple is different from the kind of pragmatic work we do at church on Sundays. Where our churches are simple and spare, our temples are layered with murals, carvings, and symbols. Where our churches are down-to-earth and plainspoken, our temples are stuffed with allusions, allegories, and sacred gestures. Growing up in the warm, shallow pools of our Sunday services may do little to prepare you for the temple's deep and bracing waters. Compared to the worn predictability of our Sunday school lessons, many members first find the temple strange. I suppose this is as it should be. The temple *is* strange. It does not belong to this world. The temple is a door and, if you pass through it, you will arrive someplace you've never been. The aim of the temple is to initiate you into the mysteries of the kingdom and before you can solve these mysteries you must encounter them as just that: unsolved mysteries.

Unveiling the mysteries of the kingdom, the temple will initiate you into what you do not know. It will acquaint you with your own ignorance. It will, with little explanation, commend to your care a series of undeciphered stories and symbols that you must neither dismiss nor explain but keep. In connection with these mysteries, you will be asked to make covenants with the Lord. You will promise to keep the commandments, practice chastity, and live the law of consecration. Here, the temple is a template: born into the undeciphered strangeness of this mortal world, our willingness to make and keep simple promises, however trying, is the thread that wends us through it. In the temple we practice wending through mystery by way of promises. Then, when we get home, we continue this same work.

Picture the temple as that vanishing point where all the world's apparently parallel lines converge. In the temple, whole worlds of people, living and dead, cross paths. Performing our rituals for our dead, we work with symbols and stories we don't quite understand for the sake of great uncles and third cousins we don't yet know. We take what is left of their lives and solemnly intertwine it with all that is available of ours. We offer our dead choices they never had, and we stand in their shoes to see more of what we've never seen.

In the Garden of Eden, God showed Adam and Eve two trees: the tree of knowledge and the tree of life. We daily eat more fruit from the first as we struggle to know good from evil. But the second tree, the tree of life, is not to be eaten but grown. In the temple, we plant the seeds of this tree and wait. We water it, tend it, and dung it. We nourish the roots and graft wild branches into it. Line by line, name by name, marriage by marriage, family by family, we gather and grow the world's family tree and seal countless generations of our dead to countless generations of children yet to be born. This work is essential. Without a welding link of some kind, the whole earth will be wasted. "We without them cannot be made perfect; neither can they without us be made perfect" because our salvation requires that "a whole and complete and perfect union, and welding together of dispensations, and keys, and powers, and glories should take place, and be revealed from the days of Adam even to the present time" (D&C 128:18).

In the temple, we are introduced to father Adam and mother Eve and, as we seal ourselves to them, God's face is revealed. The tree of life is the family tree: God is the root of that living tree and we are its branches.

Love,
A.

Eternal Life

Dear S.,

Early in section 132 of the Doctrine and Covenants, a well-known passage from the Gospel of John gets repeated, but with a twist. The passage reads: "This is eternal lives—to know the only wise and true God, and Jesus Christ, whom he hath sent" (D&C 132:24, compare John 17:3). The difference is small but compelling. Where John speaks of "eternal life," section 132 speaks of "eternal lives." What does it mean to be "eternal"? And why does "life" get changed to "lives"?

We might say that an eternal life is a life that lasts forever. But if you live forever in hell, that seems to miss the point. To have any weight, the "eternal" in "eternal life" has to amount to something more than a really long time.

In 1830, Joseph Smith and Martin Harris were told some surprising news about hell. It's true that the scriptures talk about sinners receiving eternal punishment but, the Lord cautions, this doesn't mean that their punishment is going to last forever. As the revelation puts it, "it is not written that there shall be no end to this torment, but it is written *endless torment*" (D&C 19:6). Putting *endless torment* in italics frames these words in scare quotes. The italics say: these words don't mean exactly what you think they mean. But if the "endless" torment spoken of isn't really endless, then why call it "endless torment"? Because, the revelation says, if God puts it this way, then "it is more express than other scriptures, that it might work upon the hearts of the children of men, altogether for my name's glory" (D&C 19:7).

But then the revelation shifts gears and Joseph and Martin are given a peek at what the word "eternal" might really mean. "I will explain unto you this mystery," God says (D&C 19:8). "For, behold, I am endless, and the punishment which is given from my hand is endless punishment, for Endless is my name. Wherefore—Eternal punishment is God's punishment. Endless punishment is God's punishment." (D&C 19:10–12) God doesn't intend the "eternal" of "eternal punishment" to be read as a description of how long the punishment is going to last. He intends it, borrowing on his name, to shorthand something about the *quality* of the punishment promised. Eternal punishment names the kind of punishment that comes from the hand of the Eternal One. And, more, eternal punishment is the kind of punishment that, on the cross, God himself suffered on our behalf: "For behold, I, God, have suffered these things for all, that they might not suffer if they would repent" (D&C 19:16).

If eternal punishment is God's kind of punishment, then we might, as others have, try this same reading of eternal life. Eternal life is God's kind of life. Rather than just checking a life span, "eternal" names a certain *way* of being alive, a certain way of holding life as it passes from one moment to the next. Life itself involves the passage of time and, in order to be faithful to it, we must bless rather than dam that flow. We must do as God does and allow the world and our parents and our children and our selves to grow and change and die and start again. In heaven, all the world's many parts continue moving. Being sealed to those we love doesn't seal them off from change. Rather, it binds us to them as, in their living, they never cease to change.

The law of consecration is a name for God's way of holding life as it passes. This law asks us to take everything we've been given and, of our own free will, hand it back wholesale to God. The law of consecration is an open hand. It is a certain way of receiving with open hands what God gives and returning with open hands all of the same. The law of consecration is a way of saying "yes" rather than "no" to the costs of life.

Have no doubt, these costs are high. Each of us will sacrifice everything. We will lose everyone and everything and everyplace we've ever been given. Even if we stay put and stay together, neither we nor they will stay the same. All of it will change and all of it will pass into what comes next and there is no going back. The question is, will we greet this passing with a closed fist and a hard heart or with an open palm and a consecrated life?

What is eternal life like? It's like *this*. It's like now. Eternal life is always for now and never for later. Eternal life is a certain way of holding in our hands the hunger of a human life. It is a certain way of doing whatever you're already doing. Eternal life is just like doing what you're doing right now, but doing it the way God himself would do it.

If your life seems too small and too weak to manage such a thing, you're not alone. But, in the end, that's the point: you're not alone. Remember how section 132 changes "eternal life" to "eternal lives." Every life is plural and, as a merciful result, you are never quite done and never quite your own. You will live many lives. And if you give yourself to this work, you'll find that, already, God is at work in you. Already, without your having seen, God was in there, a second life inside your life, bearing you up, giving you breath, and putting light in your eyes. Life itself depends on your filling and being filled with lives that are not your own.

Marriage will help you see this clearly. When you're sealed in the temple, you'll leave your old life on God's altar and you'll go home with two. Your life, like loaves and fishes, will be blessed and multiplied. You'll grow close, but the differences will remain. Things about your partner that used to be strange will become familiar, and things about them that used to be familiar will become strange. The person you love will always be, in part, a mystery. Love seals you together in the gathering intimacy of this inscrutability. If your love lasts, it will last because, instead of running from this strangeness, you share it. The intimacy of this strangeness, though trying, is what turns the loneliness of one eternal life into the joy of many.

When she was four, my wife sliced open her left index finger with a carving knife. She was, ambitious, trying to chop up some raw carrots while her mother wasn't looking. Her finger bled and bled and to this day it bears a wicked, hook-shaped scar. Sometimes, when I hold her hand, I feel for that scar. The other day I caught myself absently rubbing that same spot on my own hand, feeling for the ridge of that scar, and wondering where it was.

This same, strange intimacy will color your other relationships, though less vividly. You may see it with your parents and your children and your friends. You may see it with the church too. Sometimes, at church, you'll feel like a stranger wandering in a strange land. Who are these people, you'll ask, and what could you possibly have in common? In this sense, being a Mormon is not so different from being married. Sometimes when you go to church you'll see eye to eye, the pieces will fit, and you'll feel at home. But sometimes you'll just wonder and stare. Living an eternal life doesn't depend on your feeling either at home or estranged. It depends, instead, on a certain way of holding them together. Tides change, but however you happen to feel, consecrate all these feelings back to God.

What are eternal lives like? They're just like this. They're like disagreeing with your wife. They're like doing the dishes with your husband. They're like reading to your kids. They're like going to work or mowing the lawn. They're like sitting in a chair. They're like sleeping through the night or getting up before dawn. They're like visiting your mother. They're like eating a cookie. They're like being born and getting old. They're like dying.

What are eternal lives like? They, dear S., are like you.

Love,
A.

LIVING FAITH

LIVING FAITH books are for readers who cherish
the life of the mind and the things of the Spirit. Each
title is a unique example of faith in search of understanding, the voice of a scholar who has cultivated a
believing heart while engaged in the disciplines of
the Academy.